For Doctor Peter Mead
with kind and
warm words from
the author

marina ...

ANTHROPOLINGUISTIC
ASPECT OF ENGLISH POLYSEMY

MARINA ZHADEYKO

LONDON

Anthropolinguistic Aspect of English Polysemy

by Marina Zhadeyko

Institute of Humanities
Togliatti State University
14 Belorusskaya Street
Togliatti 445655
Russia

ISBN: 978-1-4461-8955-9

Published in the UK in 2010 by

Lulu Enterprises, UK Ltd
263 Putney Bridge Road
London SW15 2PU
United Kingdom
www.lulu.com

Typeset Palatino Linotype 11pt

Printed and bound in the UK by Antony Rowe Ltd, Eastbourne, East Sussex

For my parents, Nataliya and Nikoly, for obvious reasons

Contents

PREFACE 7

ACKNOWLEDGEMENTS 9

ABBREVIATIONS 10

CHAPTER 1 Word as the Object of Investigation
       1.1 Introduction 11
       1.2 Word as a Linguistic Category 13
       1.3 Meaning 16

CHAPTER 2 The General Conception of Polysemy
       2.1 Traditional Approaches to the
            Analysis of Polysemy 23
       2.2 Metaphor as a Means of Creating
            Secondary Meanings 27
       2.3 Metonymy as a Means of Creating
            Secondary Meanings 35
       2.4 Polysemy and Adjacent Notions 38

CHAPTER 3 Anthropolinguistic Aspect of Polysemy
   3.1 Introduction 51
   3.2 Anthropolinguistic Aspect of
     Metonymy 54
   3.3 Anthropolinguistic Aspect of
     Metaphor 67
   3.4 Terms 76

CONCLUSION 81

APPENDIX The List of the Obsolete Meanings,
   Extracted from the Dictionaries
   Compared 83

REFERENCES 91

Preface

This book considers the phenomenon of polysemy, and precisely the problem of semantic development of polysemous word in English. Publications on polysemy raise the questions concerning the nature of word meanings, their identification, enumeration, characteristics, the manner in which they may be related and the conceptual organization of the semantic information. Historical semantics investigating the diachronic aspect of meaning change has invented different semantic models. The problem of polysemous word has got various approaches due to diverse schools of semantics (formal or structural semantics, pragmatic semantics, and cognitive semantics). The goals of this book are to describe new results on the problem of development of polysemy in English and through the semantics of words state the possible way of evolution of human mind. We start from the hypothesis that the polysemous word makes explicit the conceptual information, which is different at different historic periods of language evolution. Historical retrospective reveals semantic changes that, in their turn, conclude the main tendency of the evolution of human cognition.

This book is aimed at students of English linguistics, taking courses in the analysis and description of the English language, post-graduates, English tutors and teachers and everyone who finds it fascinating to study the history of English words and the evolution of lexis. It is time for a new treatment of word history that will let us see changes in world interpretation hidden in word semantics. Facts used in the book are the result of the dissertation work.

Marina Zhadeyko

Acknowledgements

I gratefully acknowledge all the works, which are referred to in this book and the scholars on whose research it depends. My thanks are due to Alexandra Lavrova (Nizhny Novgorod State Linguistic University) and Siergiej Grinev-Griniewicz (Bialystok University of Finance and Management) for introducing me to anthropolinguistics and a range of problems that it deals with and for helping me with my investigation. There are also many other colleagues and friends who have contributed directly of indirectly to what this book is. Great thanks to my husband who always supports me in my writings.

Abbreviations

adj.	adjective
anat.	anatomical
ASD	Anglo-Saxon Dictionary
arch.	archaic
Du.	Dutch
esp.	especially
geom.	geometrical
Ger.	German
obs.	obsolete
OED	Oxford English Dictionary
O.N.	Old Norse (Old Icelandic)
O.S.	Old Saxon
P.Gmc.	Proto-Germanic
pl.	plural
math.	mathematical
MED	Middle English Dictionary
sing.	singular

Chapter 1

Word as the Object of Investigation

1.1 Introduction

Traditional approach to the analysis of polysemy is based on systematization of semantic changes (Ullmann, 1957; Stern, 1964; Langacker, 1968; Lyons, 1995). A new direction of science called anthropolinguistics helps to understand evolution of human cognition through the semantic development of a polysemous word. The term *anthropological linguistics* in wide sense means the study of language and society. Thus there is a range of scholars who work within this field of linguistics (Shore, 1990; Foley, 2001; Mcelhinny et al, 2003). According to Grinev-Griniewicz's (2003) approach this term got a specialized meaning designating ongoing human evolution that functions through the development of human cognition which is reflected in historical semantic changes in a language. Evolution theory might be getting a new perspective implying the transition from physical changes to mental changes.

We proceed from the fact that lexical meaning is the mental content attached to an isolated word. Thus a polysemous word in modern English can be viewed as the reflection of the result of the evolution of human thinking (Grinev-Griniewicz, 2003). The extension of existing lexical items involves both the semantic change and the change in associations. Data resulting from the diachronic investigation of the names of the parts of human body in English shows the main tendency in knowledge growth, i.e. specialization of the meaning. The progress of civilization could be viewed as a constant overcoming of semantic syncretism.

The thorough analysis of gradual semantic changes in a polysemous English word reveals the historical changes in associations from the most general to the detailed and advanced. So we have found facts supporting the idea that filogenesis of human mind follows the ontogenesis pattern.

The scientific research that has already been carried out has revealed successive historical differences in semantic organization of lexical units designating parts of human body. Investigation into the historical changes of semantic structure of nineteen polysemous words presents gradual expansion of types of associations in human cognition. The semantics of a word develops to denote new characteristic qualities of the referent which have not been realized earlier. Word dynamic structure interprets changes in the cognitive perception of the referent through semantic changes.

The semantic information of a word is a complex phenomenon organized in features that are activated and give way to new meanings. Anthropolinguistics manifests the cognitive approach. It presupposes that the semantic information pertaining to each meaning is selected by a cognitive process. The polysemy phenomenon is stated as a number of fixed meanings, listed in the lexical entry as definitions of a lexicographical entry. The meanings in the semantic structure of the word are connected derivationally sharing some semantic components. It may be a meaning core if the number of meanings is not very high. In *highly polysemous* word there are different semantic components and models, helping to explain the semantic overlap. The mechanism of semasiological change observes some historic variations.

1.2 Word as a Linguistic Category

The problems to be dealt with in the present section have attracted much scientific attention. The word as a linguistic category has been thoroughly studied by many outstanding linguists as Bloomfield, Stern and many others. According to Bloomfield (1933), a word is a form which can occur in isolation and have meaning but which cannot be analysed into elements which can all occur alone and also have meaning. However, this definition of a word is purely formal. Being a linguistic unit, word can be and is studied from different points of view. It can be defined from phonological, lexical, grammatical aspects. Scholars also consider thought as an essential part of a word. The multiplicity of aspects of every thought is also embedded in word semantics.

The question of relationship between the form and the thought or meaning is referred to as the issue of sign. As language is a system of signs then word is considered to be a sign itself. In a word, form and meaning cannot exist apart from one another. Still there is one more aspect of a sign, its interpreter that plays an important role in sign question. Different interpreters see different aspects of meaning in association with a word form and different word forms in association with a definite thought.

Linguistics studies the word as the language unit and the unit of speech. In the first case the word is seen as a part of the vocabulary system. Words are not normally used in isolation, but are combined to form units of greater magnitude. These units constitute the linguistic context in which a specific word operates. This fact gives rise to the second point of view. Words provide most of the important symbols for forming and refining thought, based on meanings that are a function of their use in discourse (Corson, 1995). So the analysis of the word involves the aspects of its meaning, depending on the context.

Nevertheless, many aspects of the matter are still very inadequately known and we cannot say that the problems are stated with precision. Since Ogden and Richards (1923) published their classic treatise on meaning there have appeared new tendencies in word study. According to Ogden-Richards's triangle (Figure 1) there are three principal elements: *symbol, thought or reference,* and *referent.* The symbol is the word that calls up the referent through the mental processes of the reference. The reference is the meaning-content of the form. The referent is the object that is perceived and that create the impression stored in the thought area.

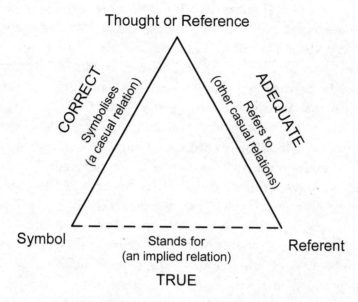

Figure 1. Ogden-Richards's triangle (Ogden & Richards, 1923)

Stephen Ullmann (1962) prefers to relabel the vertices of the triangle as *name*, *sense*, and *thing*, respectively. The connection between the form of the *name* and its *sense* is established by what is commonly referred to in semiotics as the code. The *sense* is encoded in a word, in its form. Symbolic nature of a word has some peculiarities and the most significant of them is that the word can denote objects that do not exist. The relations between such elements as *name* and *sense* are not always direct and sometimes cause ambiguity. A single form may be combined with several *senses* and the same *sense* may be combined with several word-forms. This peculiarity gives rise to several linguistic problems that of homonymy, polysemy and synonymy.

The word is characterized by arbitrariness, duality, discreteness and productivity (Lyons, 1995). The connection between the *name* and the *meaning* is arbitrary that is why association of a particular *name* with a particular *meaning* must be learned for every word independently. Duality means that words are composed of sounds which have their own principles of organization. Discreteness of the word means that it may consist of a number of morphemes and may be broken down into smaller meaningful units like eye-sight. Productivity is proved by the fact that native speakers of a language are free to act creatively to construct new meanings on the basis of well known ones.

Word is a unit that is inseparably connected with a human being. Different people assign their knowledge about the world to the word and can initiate a new idea into word semantics. Although words would be useless if only people did not share knowledge of them. Thus word cannot be studied apart from its creator, a human being.

1.3 Meaning

The correspondence between signs or words and the things that they mean is concerned by semantics. It studies the relations between things and the expressions that denote them working out schemes of representational system. Many theories of meaning see meaning as a relation between the symbols of a language and certain entities which are independent of a language. The problem of meaning including the nature of meaning, number of meanings and relations among them in a polysemous word, different aspects of word semantics, lexical ambiguity and many other minor issues has traditionally interested linguists.

There is no standard terminological distinction between *sense* and *meaning*. Some authors prefer *sense* (Cruse, 1993; Kilgarriff & Gazdar, 1995; Lyons, 2002; Ullmann, 1962) while others use *meaning* (Allwood, 2003; Janssen, 2003). Lyons defines *sense* of a word as its "place in a system of relationships which it contracts with other words in the vocabulary" (Lyons, 1995). The term *meaning* is employed in this book for what is called *reference* in Ogden-Richards' triangle and *sense* is just a component of *meaning*. The nature of word meaning has been discussed since antiquity. According to Frege meaning is reference to a real world entity. Reference, in its turn, is a relation of a signifier to a signified. The object that is referred to is an extension and the information about the object is intension. If meaning is reference, then sense is viewed as the way this reference is interpreted.

Historical approach to word study which was based on the idea that word meaning could not be split into some smaller components then has been substituted with a more advanced attitude to word meaning which is represented as a set of primitives. Structural approach to the meaning involves the analysis of its position in a system of lexical oppositions and description in terms of a network of semantic relations. With the help of analysis of various lexical oppositions within the semantic field the meaning of each lexical unit is described as a cluster of distinctive semantic features of various kinds (Bech, 1951; Coseriu, 1974). Being

17

representational system language is seen as a hierarchy with the set of basic units or primitives at its foundation which cannot be analyzed further. Componential analysis that is the basic method of structural approach has been used in cognitive linguistics as well with reference to cognitive processing.

Unlike structural approach cognitive linguistics that also deals with the problem of word meaning views this phenomenon as mental construct. Lexical items are believed to be conceptual categories that have to be studied and investigated with respect to their cognitive function. Classical description of word meaning gets a contemporary alternative in the form of prototype structure and family resemblance structure. Lexical categories mostly reveal radially-structured network characterized by central and peripheral aspects of lexical knowledge. Many cognitivists see the interaction of culture-specific knowledge and general cognitive principles as resources for semantic innovation. According to cognitive point of view, meanings have Gestalt properties and forms of meaning change are essentially based on conceptual associations of various types.

Meaning is not just a description of a part of reality but an interpretation of mental model and the mechanisms for using this model. Still there are some definite positions in this question. Meaning can be viewed as the common semantic denominator of all the word uses, as associated with functionally or biological primary instance (Rosh, 1977; Lakoff, 1987) or as potential. The meaning potential is defined as the whole information that the word has been used to convey either by a single individual or by the language community (Allwood, 2003). It includes both lexical information and encyclopaedic information. A meaning potential is activated in a context, determining the way the potential is actualized. Actualized or contextual meaning is just a part of potential. The problem of number of meanings in a word in this case does not exist since there are only different ways of activation of one and the same meaning.

The meaning of a word is assumed to consist of a variety of interrelated and interconnected senses. The semantics of a word is a complex even when relations between *name* and *meaning* are direct: one word has only one meaning. Thus *meaning* has a number of various *senses* which might be of different kinds: grammar and lexical, contextual and potential, denotative and connotative.

Word's explicit meaning is its denotation while ideas implied by the word and not directly indicated form its connotation. For example, Lyons defines the denotation of a lexeme as "the relationship that holds between that lexeme and persons, things, places and other entities external to the language system" (Lyons, 1995). A large number of words also carry some extra associations, often personal or emotional that the use of the word brings to mind. Connotation is usually associated with stylistic peculiarities of word usage and its synonymous relations. Synonyms are seen as the words with the same denotation but different connotation. Yet denotation and connotation are both important to determine word meaning not only in a given context but in language system as well.

Many words incorporate an evaluative element as a part of their connotative meaning. Thus the word is not only the symbol that refers us to some entity in a real world but it also expresses speaker's emotions, feelings towards it and arose them in listener. Sometimes words are used for evaluative purposes only like the word *disgusting*. So in cases like this the evaluative meaning prevails over the denotative meaning of a word or even acts alone. This evaluative element may be negative (derogative) or, on the contrary, positive. For example, *mouth* in the meaning *a silly person, a dupe* (1680) is negative, but the same word in the meaning *one who speaks on behalf of another; a spokesman* (1563) is positive.

Variation in meaning gives rise to some particular problems. The problem of meaning is closely connected with that of homonymy and polysemy. Still the account for these phenomena may be different. For instance, the issue of distinguishing polysemy and homonymy has got different approaches. On the one hand, these two phenomena have been long distinguished on the basis of some reasonable criteria such as historical criterion, the part of speech criterion and the criterion of different inflectional paradigms. According to the first criterion, coalescence of two historically distinct linguistic forms results in homonymy. Homonymous are the lexical units appeared by the process of conversion and the meanings of one and the same word, associated with different inflectional paradigms.

On the other hand, traditional linguistic criteria sometimes turn out to be insufficient. Since homonymy obtains when two words accidentally have the same form, the verbs derived from nouns by the process of conversion are still semantically connected with them, having the same historical origin and therefore cannot be regarded as homonymous. In this case a wider notion of polysemy can be adopted ignoring the part of speech criterion. The question of the criterion's importance is taken into consideration and thus we see that the criteria are not equal. In the case with the conversion we realize the semantic connection, but there are cases which do not reveal any connection at the level of semantics nowadays. Only the etymological analysis shows the fact that the words treated as homonymous have the same historical origin. For instance, the traditional example of homonymy **bank** as *financial institution* and **bank** as *land along the side of a river* turns out to be a case of historical polysemy as they are derived from old French **banc** *bench*.

Thus the problem of distinguishing homonymy and polysemy has historical and contemporary aspects. Consequently there can be two different points of view. For ordinary people guided by intuition of distinctness of meaning it is right to treat such a pair as homonymous while some linguists, taking into consideration the historical criterion, see polysemous relations in the last analysis. Anyway, it remains an open question whether any of the above mentioned criteria of distinguishing homonymy and polysemy has more importance than the rest if each of them can be ignored. Even the semantic characterization can be too abstract or general in some cases. And as we have seen the ignorance of this or that criterion depends on the definite case. Anyway, the issue of distinguishing homonymy and polysemy is a lexicological problem as there is very little ambiguity in words used in speech chain.

Meaning is linguistic knowledge while concepts are knowledge of the world. Word meaning is the language reflection of interpretation of a piece of reality. Interpretation of reality is the psychic process subjected to historical development. This development might be of individual character and conventional one as well. We change our personal attitude to the world around us during our life and as a consequence start realizing new aspects of surrounding objects. The same thing happens to mankind in the historical development. New ideas, facts, discoveries then cumulate in a language. Thus the semantic evolution of a word leads to actualization of the elements of cognitive structure. Word meanings correspond to concepts, mental or cognitive constructs created in connection with experience.

Associations, building the semantics of a word, are partly universal and partly specific to particular languages. The world is interpreted through the language we use and this has some influence on the perception. Still there are some characteristics of the real objects we realize throughout the word.

Chapter 2
The General Conception of Polysemy

2.1 Traditional Approaches to the Analysis of Polysemy

The term polysemy, designating the existence of two or more meanings in a word, was coined by Breal (1924). Since that time polysemy has become one of the traditional linguistic categories investigated by scholars all over the world. Still actual are questions of development of polysemy, universal mechanisms of the semantic change that result in polysemy, semantic structure of a polysemous word, the existence of *general meaning* of a polysemous word and many others.

Polysemous relations are studied synchronically and diachronically. Synchronically word is realized as a network of meanings while diachronically we distinguish secondary meanings from primary ones. Based on the idea of stability, synchronic research of polysemous word structure reveals semantic constants. These constants being parts of the meanings form centres of variability. For example, the lexical unit **body** has the following meanings which share the constant invariant component – *the main part of some object*:

a) the main part of a man or animal, without the head, arms and legs;
b) the part of a vehicle fitted to receive the load;
c) the hull of a ship;
d) the main stem, trunk, stock of a plant or tree;
e) the main portion of a document.

The same word *body* also has another group of meanings united by the semantic component – *an assemblage of units*:

a) the nation in its corporate character; the state;
b) an organized collection of fighting men acting together; a force;
c) a comprehensive and systematic collection of the details of any subject; an arranged whole of information; hence, a pandect;
d) government; a society, association, league, fraternity.

In such cases the limit of variation is seen in the qualitative modification of word semantic structure which is observed in the formation of new centre of variability.

Discussing polysemy diachronically various types of *extension* or *transference* of meaning are recognized. Among these types metaphorical extension and metonymy have been thoroughly studied to state the basic mechanisms for transitive alternations. Other changes involve a widening and narrowing of meaning. There are some traditional examples of relations between the earlier and the later meaning of a word in textbooks on semantics. For instance, *deer*, originally designating *any animal*, was narrowed down then to a definite species in the meaning *a graceful animal, the male of which has horns*. Widening of a historical meaning can be exemplified by the verb **sail**, first meaning *go by sailing vessel* and later on *go by any sea-going vessel*. The relation between a meaning denoting *a fibre* like in the word **cotton** and a meaning denoting *a thread made from that fibre* is that of metonymy. Metaphorical shift is that based on some resemblance between the reference of the primary meaning and that of the secondary one as in the case with **face** which means not only *the front of the head*, but also *a surface*. It is obvious that the direction of interest and the emphasis on certain aspects of meaning change are largely determined by the concept of meaning which individual authors and schools of thought embrace.

A permanent connection between the word and the new meaning happens when the incidental use becomes habitual. Such changes are adopted by the whole speaking community and registered in dictionaries. This means that the change has been incorporated in the language system of the group. Still the historical theory cannot account for these natural processes in a natural way and they are usually treated as deviations from the norm. Thus the problem of semantic development of a word requires further investigation.

Change of meaning is identified as habitual modification (Stern, 1964; Lehrer & Lehrer, 1995). We have a change of meaning when a word is employed to express a meaning which it has not previously expressed (Stern, 1964). There are different ways of formalizing polysemous relations starting with *directions in linguistic space* and ending with the code based on formal links (Kilgarriff & Gazdar

1995). Metalanguage as a means of investigation of polysemous relations is becoming more and more popular. Still metalanguage does not contribute much to the explanation of change of meaning. One should not confuse mechanisms and causes of semantic change. The patterns of use called mechanisms (e.g. metaphor, metonymy, euphemisms etc.) indicate the possible paths of change (Geeraerts, 1997), whereas a cause indicates why one of these possibilities is realized by a speaker (Geeraerts, 1997).

Systematic and partial regularity of the range of polysemous relations is one of the scientists' concerns (Apresjan, 1974; Kilgarriff & Gazdar, 1995). Apresjan (1974) coined the term *regular polysemy*. He employed this term for cases of polysemy where the same relationship holds between the meanings for two or more polysemous words. *Regular polysemy* is traditionally connected with routine patterns of metonymic extension. For instance, the relationship between a meaning denoting *a fibre* like in the word *silk* and a meaning denoting *a garment made from that fibre* is true for a group of polysemous units. The primary meaning of a word forms definite possibilities and limits for alternations. On the basis of diachronic investigations definite abstract conceptual models of metonymy such as **author for work authored, container for contained** have been stated. The valuable contributions of Kilgarriff and Gazdar (1995) are more concerned with exploration of the formal structure of the regularities.

Studying relations between the separate meanings of a polysemous word is traditionally based on topological scheme, revealing the direction of semantic derivation. On

26

the grounds of topological scheme there differentiated radial, chain and mixed structure of a polysemous word. Structure of a polysemous word let differentiate such kinds of polysemy as monocentral, polycentral and syncretic (McKnight, 1923). The change of meaning regards not only onomasiological level, but also its semasiology.

Polysemy as language reflection of conceptualization and categorization of reality is studied by cognitive theory, taking into consideration not only characteristics of word's semantics, but also features of man's linguacreative activity. In this case the meaning of a word is understood not as a set of characteristics, necessary for the identification of an object only, but as the whole complex of knowledge about the referent. Changes in semantic structure of a word are considered to be reflection of conceptual derivation. Historical modification of word's semantics explicates changes in the processes of conceptualization and categorization.

2.2 Metaphor as a Means of Creating Secondary Meanings

Metaphor and metonymy are claimed to be the main sources of lexical polysemy. Metaphor is a complicated and multi-aspectual phenomenon what explains long interest to its studying (Black, 1962). The character of metaphor researches registers logic-philosophical, linguistic, lexicographical and cognitive-psychological approaches (Richards, 1936; Pierce, 1958; Cassirer, 1977; Bachelard,

1978). The history of metaphor studying and conceptual nature of this phenomenon defined metaphor as the subject-matter of a new interdisciplinary field of knowledge, called metaphorology.

The first clearly formulated definition of metaphor and its main function to find resemblance belongs to Aristotle. In antique, classical and cognitive linguistics the definition of metaphor is based on the acknowledgement of resemblance between two referents when the meaning is transferred. For instance, *lip* in the meaning *one of the edges of a wound* (1400) is a result of metaphorical transition from the historical meaning *either of the two fleshy structures which in man and other animals form the edges of the mouth* (1000) on the basis of visual analogy that is explicit in the semantic metaphor mediator *the edges of.*

Originally metaphor was considered as a literary device used for imaginative phrases in poetry and literature. In Greek metaphor was one of powerful devices for argumentation and rhetorical method. The deviant use of a word, underlined by many different theories as one of the basic features of metaphor, accounts for traditional exclusion of metaphor from descriptive and scientific discourse. Metaphor is defined as giving something a name that properly belongs to something else. Differentiation between language metaphor and metaphor as a stylistic device is grounded on the loss of imagery and going of the meaning out of the context. There is no principle difference in the way these kinds of metaphor are created. Being the most typical means of semantic development of a word, metaphor differs from other means by the prevalence of image associations in the process of *knowledge transition* (Langacker, 1968; Goodman, 1981).

Metaphor is also regarded as a calculated category mistake – or rather as a happy and revitalizing, even if bigamous, second marriage (Goodman, 1981). Category mistake forming the basis of metaphor defined as the break of semantic norm let unite distinct notions, ideas in the semantics of one and the same word, giving birth to polysemy (Ryle, 1949; Bickerton, 1969). For example, *lappet* as *a part of anything that hangs loose* (1677) is a result of metaphorical extension of the meaning *a loose or overlapping part of a garment, forming a flap or fold* (1573). Thus metaphor is a flexible device for extending the resource of the language and it is also seen as a method for assimilating new knowledge into the old.

Regular patterns of metaphor expansion similar in national metaphor systems of the bearers of different cultures in one historic period and the bearers of one culture in different historic periods have lead to the recognition of metaphor as language universal (Ullmann, 1962). Universal character of metaphor is explained by a common biological and psychological origin of people, universal language function, universal cognitive mechanism and universal mechanism of creating metaphors in language. One of such universals is the metaphorical projection **concrete** → **abstract**. It is considered that thinking about the abstract concept is facilitated by the more concrete concept.

The presence of definite systematic regularities in the basis of metaphor let us reveal the mechanisms of metaphor expansion and principles of classification for metaphor typology. Diversity of semantic kinds of metaphor is caused by semantic mediator between the original and transferred meanings. The issue of dual meaning for metaphor is closely connected with the question of the structure of the metaphor. In the literature on metaphor different terminology is used to interpret the mechanism of this phenomenon. Richards (1936) introduced two terms *tenor* and *vehicle* for discussing metaphor. Under the *tenor* he sees the underlying idea or principle subject and under *vehicle* he understands what is metaphorically attributed to the *tenor*. Beardsley, in his turn, uses the *subject* and the *modifier* instead of the *tenor* and the *vehicle*. The *modifier's* connotations are what attributed to the *subject*.

According to other more detailed views metaphor is divided into *tenor*, *vehicle* and *ground*. The first two are still seen as in Richards' terminology and the *ground* is a set of features that *tenor* and *vehicle* have in common. A set of associated ideas and beliefs that are common to the primary and the secondary subjects forms the "bridge" between the two domains. According to the number of features, defining the analogy of referents, metaphors are divided into one-componental and multi-componental ones. Examples may be the meanings of the word **heart**. **Heart** – *the hollow muscular or otherwise contractile organ which, by its dilatation and contraction, keeps up the circulation of the blood in the vascular system of an animal* (1000) motivated the meaning *the innermost or central part of anything: the centre, middle* (1310). The ground for derivation is the definite *placement* of the **heart** in a human body. Thus the *placement* is the only component that is shared by both meanings of

30

the word so the metaphor is one-componential in this case. The example of multi-componential metaphor is observed in the structure of the word *back* that has the meaning *the outer edge of a rainbow* (1450) appeared on the basis of the meaning *the convex surface of the body of man and vertebrate animals which is adjacent to the spinal axis, and opposite to the belly and the front or face* (885). In this case not only the *placement* is shared by two meanings but the *shape of the bending back* as well.

Every metaphor conveys some new semantic content since the true conditions for things compared are different. This new semantic content reveals the asymmetry of metaphor. The structure of metaphor gives rise to differentiation metaphors into sensor and rational. Sensor metaphors are based on human feelings, visual and sound perception, touch and taste. For example, *finger – one of the five terminal members of the hand* (950) motivated the secondary meaning *a finger-like projection; esp. such a part either of the fruit, foliage, or root of a plant* (1702), which reflects the preference of visual similarities between the objects. Rational metaphors are different in associations since they reveal mostly functional and structural features of the objects. For example, *chest – a box, a coffer; now mostly applied to a large box of strong construction, used for the safe custody or articles of value* (700) gave birth to the meaning *the place in which the money belonging to a public institution is kept; treasury, coffer* (1558). The secondary meaning registers functional characteristics ignoring visual features typical for historical meaning.

However, sensor and rational peculiarities may be combined in a metaphorical meaning. In the semantics of the word **hand** – *the terminal part of the arm beyond the wrist, consisting of the palm and five digits* (825) there appeared metaphorical meaning *prehensile claw or chela in crustaceans, and formerly to the tarsus of the anterior leg in insects* (1382) which is based on the complex of visual and functional characteristics of the historical referent. Human beings see analogies with them in everything that surrounds them, generating properties which are relevant to humans and other objects of reality.

Eventually, many scientists have treated metaphor as if it appears with two ideas to be contrasted and compared. The idea of hidden comparison accounts for substitution point of view on metaphor. According to which a metaphorical expression is used instead of an equivalent literal expression and, therefore, can be replaced by its literal counterpart. On the other hand, metaphors also involve some form of literal falsity and, as a consequence, the understanding of metaphorical meaning requires resolving this anomaly. In this case metaphor is considered to be some kind of puzzle that, in its turn, brings new life to old words. In fact, nature of metaphor is that of complex of something contrasted and similar. On the basis of comparison of features shared by two pieces of reality new associations arise and contribute to the more precise understanding of the surroundings. Thus on the grounds of comparison of something belonging to different categories human cognition finds similarities.

The individual skill at half-revealing the meaning and that one at motivating the hearer to resolve the conflict gives birth to metaphorical expressions which, in due course, become conventional. Thus the status of metaphor develops from that of ornamentation when an author chooses metaphorical expression to make his speech fancier and more appealing to that accepted in society. When metaphor appears for the first time its associations are new to people since an author has presented his individual interpretation of a piece of reality. His idea then is becoming more and more spread and people get used to this new analogy. Author metaphor is now seen as a usual way of interpretation of a piece of reality and people using it in their speech see more similarity than difference between the ideas forming the basis of metaphor. Trite metaphors fixed in dictionaries mark associations conventionalized in society. This is the last stage in metaphor development at which people do not realize the metaphoric character of nomination any more hence they are called trite metaphor.

The analysis of metaphor mechanisms shows semantic changes in a word when it develops a transferred meaning like in the case with *attic – small room just under the roof of a house* when there appears the metaphoric meaning *head of a human being*. Marginal connotative elements of historical meaning form the ground for new associations included into word semantics. Metaphorization is often accompanied by the process of derogation like in the words *clam, flytrap, gash, rat-trap* denoting *mouth*. The estimation in a metaphor reveals the presence of the emotional component in the structure of metaphor. The above examples contain more emotional charge than literal expression. The emotive tension is definitely observed in genuine metaphors. Once a new connection is established between previously unrelated ideas it causes feelings of surprise and tension but then the associations seem no longer surprising. In trite metaphors the degree of emotional import has been reduced.

To understand metaphorization as a systematic process the issue of relation between word meaning and human cognition needs to be illuminated. Thus contemporary theories of metaphor rather account for cognitive content of metaphor than its emotional import. The development of anthropologically oriented methods of research has contributed to a new metaphor theory, based on the idea that metaphor is a verbalized way of human thinking (Turner & Fauconnier, 2000). The ability of metaphor to classify reveals the way human experience is organized. Metaphor creates the definite paradigm, represented by speech, language and conceptual elements. Metaphorical character of human thinking, claimed by cognitive linguistics, forms the system of invariant conceptual metaphors such as orientational, ontological and structural (Lakoff, 1987). Among structural metaphors there differentiated anthropomorphical, zoomorphological, military, political ones and their variants in the form of language nominations.

Metaphors are grounded in our culture and our experience of physical world. The knowledge of the world is encoded in metaphors as well as in other language structures. Today the issue of knowledge representation is the central problem in language studies. Cognitive theory of metaphor studies the correlations between mental structures and the way they are interpreted verbally. Conceptual metaphors are seen as the system of units which can be analyzed further into smaller components out of which knowledge representation can be built. Conceptual metaphors are open dynamic structures that can reflect the process of knowledge acquisition and integration of new information with the existing knowledge. Analysis of conceptual metaphors required the working out meta-language. The meta-language is knowledge about the way knowledge of the piece of world is represented in conceptual metaphors.

The research of conventional system of metaphors reveals the mental mapping of reality and argues that conceptual metaphors are kept in human cognition (Lakoff, 1987). In contemporary approach to metaphor it is seen as a mode of thought not as a figure of speech.

2.3 Metonymy as a Means of Creating Secondary Meanings

Metonymy is an expression that basically refers to one entity and then indicates some other entity associated with the original in a given domain. It is a particular source of meaning change in a polysemous word. Traditional rhetorical study of the metonymy as speech ornament let state the fundamental characteristic of this phenomenon, defined as transference grounded on adjacency. Adjacency in metonymy is seen by linguists as the result of contiguity of objects in space and time. Transference of names in metonymy does not involve a necessity for two different words to have a common component in their semantic structures as in the case with metaphor but proceeds from the fact that two phenomena have common grounds of existence in reality.

Metonymy exists in conceptual mental system as a cognitive model, characterized by the relations of substitution between the components as in the word **breech**, used for dress nomination – *a garment covering the loins and thighs* and the part of human body – *the part of the body covered by this garment*. Metonymy is seen as one of the key mechanisms of conceptualization and following it process of categorization. Logical approach to the study of metonymy explains the phenomenon in logical operations, forming the ground of semantic shift. Being one of the sources of polysemy metonymy unlike metaphor reflects objective relationship between objects and phenomena in reality. Being the linguistic reflection of the act of indirect reference metonymy is opposed to metaphor on the grounds of semantic basis. It is noticed that with the increase of abstraction of word semantics the possibility of metaphorical expansion is narrowed down to its minimum, whereas the part of metonymy grows (Lakoff, 1987; Turner & Fauconnier, 2000).

Logical-rhetorical approach reveals the connection between metonymy and metaphor, defining them as a result of doubling of synecdoche. Metonymy is also seen as a special case of metaphor such as the word *finger* in the meaning *one who supplies information or indicates victims to criminals* (1962). This secondary meaning is based on the relations between the part, *one of the five terminal members of the hand* (950), and the whole, *person*, revealing the similarity of function "to indicate". In this case the complex model of metonymy **property** → **part of the body** → **person** is realized. In metaphorical substitutions some linguists identify metonymical practical ground, based on the use of physical and functional properties of the primary referent of a word like in a case with *banana* meaning not only *a long, yellow, sweet fruit,* but also *the part of the face just above the mouth* on the basis of metonymical abstraction of "fruit shape". Metonymical ground is typical for metaphors, used to reflect emotions on the basis of behaviour and physiological reactions to them.

Metonymy is considered in this book as a universal process of development of word semantics. Linguistic theory of metonymy covers the study of semantic mechanisms of metonymical expansion and the typology of these mechanisms, analysis of peculiarities of nominative, adjective and verbal metonymy. It is argued that typicalness of metonymical models in a polysemous word depends on belonging of a word to the definite semantic group. For example, according to the dictionaries *eye, ear, nose, foot, mouth* and others denote *the part of the body* and *its function.* So *tongue – an organ, possessed by man and by most vertebrates, occupying the floor of the mouth, often protrusible and freely movable* (897) and also *the faculty of speech; the power of articulation or vocal expression or description; voice; speech; words, language* (890). One more example of regular metonymy is observed in the model **part of the body** → **article (part) of clothes** represented in the semantics of the following words: *breast, skull, thigh, toe, waist, wrist* and many others of the same semantic group.

The semantic shift **part** ↔ **whole** is regarded to be the basic model of metonymy, determined by fundamental property of human consciousness. At conceptual level **part** ↔ **whole** manifests the relationship **concept** ↔ **domain** since every concept might become the ground for other concepts.

Sometimes it is rather difficult to classify the type of a shift in the structure of a polysemous word since vagueness between the meanings. For example, *arm – the upper limb of the human body, from the shoulder to the hand* (950) is also known in the meaning *the arm of the armchair*. From the semantics of the word it is clear that the relations between these meanings may be classified as metaphorical and metonymical as well. From the metaphorical point of view both meanings share the idea of *side placement* whereas metonymy is observed in contiguity of objects in space: the human *arms* rest on *the arms of the armchair*. Impossibility to differentiate metaphor from metonymy in such cases let consider them as the result of cooperative simultaneous activity of metonymy and metaphor. These linguistic entities form the complex unit which is named either metaphorical metonymy or metonymical metaphor.

2.4 Polysemy and Adjacent Notions

Being a linguistic phenomenon polysemy is closely connected with homonymy and syncretism. Syncretism is a confusing concept. In linguistics there are different points of view on semantic syncretism. Some scholars claim that originally undifferentiated syncretic formations appear in languages and later language development shows the splitting of the semantic unity. The same idea accounts for the genetic grounds of parts of speech. Others believe that the creation of wide generic and abstract meanings is the result of later evolution of the language.

Defining syncretism as conjugation, undifferentiating characteristic to the initial stage of development of something one assumes that the development of civilization is connected to gradual neutralization of syncretism. Syncretism as hidden word polysemy is not realized by contemporaries what means that some notions are not differentiated like in the Old English *hyge* meaning *mind, heart, pride*. Obviously different ideas were united in the semantics of one and the same Old English word. Such examples let us see the associations typical for people who lived long ago.

Reconstruction of hypothetic roots of the Indo-European and Germanic languages on the basis of phonetic correlations and closeness of meanings gives many ancient examples with abstract semantics like **kenk – to burn, fire, soul >* the Old English *knecca – neck*. Evolution of human society has reflected in historically modified picture of the world the dynamism of which is caused by differences in world perception by human beings in different epochs (Trier, 1931).

The semantics of the ancient word says about undifferentiated perception of objects and their characteristics, inseparability of abstract from concrete and individual from general. For instance, the semantic structure of the Old English word *fæðm* (fathom) included the meanings *embracement, heart, soul, breast, bottom*. Under syncretism some scholars mean the direct link between the definite object and its characteristic reflecting the way of world interpretation of people lived long ago. This way of thinking is also connected with mythological perception of surroundings. Mythological thinking is characterized by inability of human mind at earlier stages of the history of evolution to single a human being out of nature. The unity of a human being and nature in the mind of a person at an earlier historical stage is being seen through the analysis of the semantics of words denoting parts of human body which also designate natural phenomena. For example, the Old English word *sweora* meant *neck* and also denoted *the declination of a mountain near the summit; the most level spot between two hills* and *the part where the distance between opposite shores is least*.

In the Old English there are also words of generic semantics denoting several notions united by the same idea. The word with the semantic dominant is defined as a lexical unit with broad semantics. The Old English word *heafod* (head) was used for nomination of rising grounds of the spatial objects like *the commencing point or the highest point of a stream, of a field, hill, etc.* (847). Syncretism as well as polysemy may mean a number of meanings in a word structure, but the link character between them is different. The main difference between polysemy and historical syncretism is the delimitation of notions in the language system that is proved by the disjunction of meanings. In the Old English the abstract meaning was not completely separated from the concrete one that is seen in the definitions given in historical dictionaries.

The acknowledgement of syncretism through the comparison of the same fact of the language at different historical stages, taking into consideration that language development led to differentiation of formerly united meanings, requires the working out of appropriate methods. Only the approach that takes into account the phenomenon of polysemy let us reconstruct the changes in the system of world interpretation since historical elements may keep in word structure. Under differentiation of formerly united notions scholars traditionally see their different nomination in modern language. For example, lexicographic sources register the usage of *nose* in the meaning *an elephant's trunk* till the 17th century. In the case of polysemy when the historical meaning keeps in the semantic structure of the word it seems possible to use anthropological analysis.

Diachronic analysis reveals the changes in the models of derivation at different stages of development of polysemy and shows the historic depth of the model of derivation. For example, the metonymic model **whole → part** has been fixed by lexicographic sources since the Middle Ages. Thus the word **gum** historically meant *indifferently for the inside of the mouth or throat* (825). During the period of the Middle Ages the evolution of the word semantics is due to the meaning *the firm fleshy integument of the jaws and bases of the teeth; also said of the toothless jaw and its integument; also sing. the portion of the integument attached to a single tooth* (1398). Other historic periods add new meanings to the semantics of the word.

The suggestion that the historic syncretism serves as a basis for the development of polysemy is proved by the experiment on chronological stability of a word. During the experiment it was stated that a great number of meanings in the historic past secures chronological stability of a word. The most dramatic percent of meanings' obsolesce is registered among the words with one meaning only like the Old English *lichama* while all the words with six and more historical meanings like *side* have kept in the language.

The evolution of lexical system of the language supposes the following order: **syncretism → polysemy → semantic homonymy**. In the aspect of prototype semantics it is proved that the most part of Indo-European homonymy is originated from the former polysemy. In due course of history there is a tendency to the increase of language abilities to differentiate and to the decrease of the number of words with undifferentiated meanings.

First transferred meanings of the word *elbow* denoted *angles* and *bends* and only in 1877 dictionaries register the meaning *the conical hollow in the bottom of a wine-bottle*. This new meaning is motivated by the realization of the characteristic *the shape of the elbow when it is bent*. The appearance of a new motivation base supports the idea that our interpretation of the world is becoming more and more precise through the history of mankind.

Evolution of polysemy may lead to the split of semantic connection between the word meanings. Such cases may even be registered by dictionaries as homonyms. Thus *ear* (a) denotes *the organ of hearing in men and animals* and other referents while *ear* (b) *the action of ploughing*. In this example the split is caused by the obsolescence of the meaning *a fastened beam on either side of the head of a plough produces an ear* in the semantic structure of the word *ear*. Phenomena of polysemy and homonymy are in the relationship of intersection that greatly broadens the theory of homonymy. According to this point of view homonyms can be meanings of a polysemous word which reveal no common semantic features between them.

If syncretism is typical for the initial stage of lexis development of a language and polysemy is the result of the developing system we can state that polysemy neutralizes syncretism. Some linguists refuse the idea that syncretism is typical for the initial stage of lexis development of the language. They believe that syncretism is typical for the initial and modern stages of language development. In this case under semantic syncretism they understand the unity of several structural semantic components of different levels of abstraction difficult to unite or the neutralization of polar ideas.

The analysis of the words of modern English shows connected and simultaneously actualized components in the semantics of syncretic units. *Finger* in the meaning *one who supplies information or indicates victims to criminals* (1962) representing a bundle of semantic components reflects the unity of different levels of abstraction (*person* and *function of the part of the body*). In modern language key words characteristic to the given society in the given epoch are also considered as syncretic units. Usually semantic structure of syncretic unit both in the ancient and modern languages is characterized by the absence of successive derivation in the hierarchy of structural elements. While the resource of polysemy is semantic derivation, syncretism is caused by conjugation. Registration of several meanings in a word in the Old English dating the same time does not let reconstruct the direction of semantic derivation. For example, in the Old English *fæðm* (fathom) represented two meanings *the embracing arms; bosom* (1000) and *grasp, power* (1000) which show no derivational connection. So we can see this word as a syncretic unit.

The question of proper interpretation of semantic processes has not got the direct answer. Being important for modern lexicography the problem of differentiation between polysemy and homonymy is characterized by inconsistency of lexicographic interpretation. For example, in the Oxford Advanced Learner's Dictionary of Current English (Hornby, 2001) *cheek* is represented in two meanings: *the side of the face below the eye* and *impudence; saucy speech or behaviour*. The English-Russian Dictionary (Mednikova & Apresian, 1993) treats *cheek* as *the side of the face below the eye* and *cheek* as *impudence* as homonyms.

Being universal feature of natural languages, polysemy is one of the main characteristics of modern English language that differentiates it from other languages. More than 58% of words in the English language registered by Roget's thesaurus (Lloyd, 1982) are polysemous. Whereas the polysemy is determined by the nature of language as psychic entity, homonymy is not the absolute universal, but a linguistic tendency. Wide spread of homonymy in the system of the English language is caused by the exis-

44

tence of a great number of phonetic complexes belonging to different parts of speech. For example, *breast* is registered as a noun, verb and an adjective in dictionaries. This kind of homonymy is caused by structural synchronous links between mentioned parts of speech and semantic closeness that is not typical for homonymy.

In some lexicographic sources homonyms created with the help of conversion are seen as one and the same language unit functioning as a noun and a verb simultaneously (Ogata, 1943). This approach comes into contradiction with the concept of the word as a language unit belonging to the definite lexico-grammatical group. In the appendix to A Concise Etymological Dictionary of the English Language (Skeat, 1909) there are no registered cases of partial lexico-grammatical homonymy connected with conversion. However, in the dictionary they are considered as pairs of separate words *chin (noun)* and *chin (verb)* (Skeat, 1909). Preservation of semantic connection between the parts of speech by conversion and the field nature of parts of speech let consider this kind of homonymy within the integral conception of polysemy and define it either as lexico-grammatical type of polysemy or intercategorial polysemy. Word ability to unite two and more categorical meanings is admitted by many linguists.

The integral conception dramatically broadens the notion of polysemy due to taking into consideration grammatical level of the language. This conception is based on the projection of one and the same lexical unit on the three planes – adjective, noun and verb ones. Differentiation of integral polysemy from homonymy is carried out on the base of preservation of semantic. Considering homonyms etymologically different words like *temple – the flat part on either side of the head between the forehead and the ear* (1310) and *temple – a building used for the worship of a god* (825), having become identical in pronunciation thanks to phonetic reasons, is not relevant in the aspect of synchrony. In this case polysemy and homonymy are considered as two poles apart. There is a scale with an amount of transition cases between these poles. Reduction and further split of semantic connection between the meanings of the polysemous word as a result of a link meaning loss leads to appearance of semantic homonyms (Ullmann, 1957). One of the markers of homonym development is grammar transformation like plural form of a word *jaw* required in the meaning *the seizing action or capacity of any devouring agency, as death, time* (1563).

Phenomenon of homonymy connected with breaking of word sense identity demonstrates prevalence of difference over identity in contrast to prevalence of identity over difference characteristic for polysemy. In this case differentiation between polysemy and homonymy is due not to polar opposition but the degree of semantic closeness between meanings. Homonymy, in contrast to polysemy, is acknowledged a correlative category, since it requires correlation of a word with another to admit it as a homonym. Hence the unit of homonymy is a homonymous row, not a separate word as in the case of polysemy.

The problem of differentiation of polysemy from homonymy is traditional for linguistic studies. Dealing with this problem leads to working out semantic, structural, syntactic and word formation criteria including criterion of a synonymous row and also the method of coordinative analysis. The use of formal criteria does not show objective results, because of identity of formal characteristics of homonyms and polysemous words. Both homonyms and meanings of a polysemous word are characterized by differences in lexical and syntactical combinations, entering different synonymous, word formation and theme groups.

Admitting word formation criterion as the essential for differentiation polysemy from homonymy by some linguists is refused by others on the basis of existence of different derivatives belonging to one and the same denotation and different word formation rows of the meanings of a polysemous word. For example, the polysemous word *lobe* in the meaning *the lower rounded end of the ear* motivates the derivative *lobeless*, while the meaning *any projecting part of an organ* forms the units like *lobed, lobectomy, lobulate*.

The use of coordinative analysis without taking into account the semantic criteria does not show trustworthy results of differentiation polysemy from homonymy while the use of other methods in case of the same words leads to different results. Homonymy of relations registered by the method of coordinative analysis must be correlated to the degree of semantic closeness between the meanings in the structure of a polysemous word. The breaking off coordination reveals the meanings, which do not have common semantic features. Inability of formal methods to solve the problem of differentiation polysemy from homonymy makes us turn to psycholinguistic experiment, orientated towards native speakers' intuition. Appreciation of the degree of semantic closeness of words due to eleven points scale let state transitional cases between polysemy and homonymy.

The try to find criteria, proving the presence or absence of semantic connection between the meanings of one and the same phonetic sequence, has advanced semantic criterion. Acknowledgement of semantic criterion priority as a means of differentiation polysemy from homonymy is based on the use of common components of dictionary definitions or lexical prototype. The second is claimed universal criterion what leads to direct solution without consideration of derivational and etymological criteria.

The essential features of polysemy are typicality, directness and metonymy of connections between meanings. Metaphor is seen as a notion close to homonymy and even identified with it. Still other scholars claim that metaphorical secondary meaning is semantically much closer connected and shows fewer tendencies to the formation of homonymy. This is explained by radial type of connection typical to metaphorization. In this case words revealing chain connection between the meanings are seen as closest to homonymy, because they demonstrate less degree of semantic connection cohesion. However, features seen as typical for polysemy are sometimes in contrast to the definition of polysemy phenomenon and not taken into consideration. Hence the problem of differentiation polysemy from homonymy requires a complex approach, revealing different aspects in relationships between separate meanings and the words which sound identically.

Acknowledging homonymy as the limit of polysemy

development correlates with the negation of bilateral connection between these phenomena, reflected in the birth of polysemy on the basis of homonymy. One of the examples of the birth of polysemy on the basis of homonymy may be the cases of the so-called folk etymology like the word *shock* in the expressions *shock of corn* and *shock of hair*. Speakers of the English language reinterpreted *shock* in the expressions *shock of hair* according to analogy with another common word of the phrases *shock of corn*. Historically *shock of hair* comes from *shough* (1599), the name for the type of dog, "lap dog having long, shaggy hair", which was said to have been brought originally from Iceland. The word is perhaps from an O.N. variant of *shag* whereas *shock* in *shock of corn* is from P.Gmc. **skukka-* (cf. O.S. *skok*, Du. *schok* "sixty pieces", Ger. *Hocke* "heap of sheaves"). Establishment of such relations of lexical motivation between etymologically not connected units, leading to an appearance of a polysemous word with heterogenic etymology, is interpreted as remotivation. Differentiation of the meanings of a polysemous word and homonyms, essential for lexical system of a language, is not relevant in the case of description of human speech skills. Since a language bearer precepts separate word meanings as homonymous word forms.

Chapter 3

Anthropolinguistic Aspect of Polysemy

3.1 Introduction

In June 2004 at the international conference "Language and Culture" in Bialystok, Poland there was Manifesto on new linguistic approach, anthropolinguistic, signed. Peculiarity of this scientific approach is in concentration of attention on the evolution of human cognition and the reflection of this process in lexis.

The data of etymological and diachronic researches and the growing interest to the problem of revealing principles of thinking gave rise to anthropolinguistic approach or anthropolinguistics. Anthropolinguistic research is based on the correlation of filogenetic facts with ontogenetic data. According to some experimental results the level of conceptual development of the individual can affect metaphoric understanding. The pattern of metaphoric comprehension in children seems to follow the evolution of their semantic domains. These facts are supported by the results of terminological researches in linguistics. Registration of anthropolinguistic aspect in a language is based on systematic diachronic analysis of lexis from different fields of knowledge. The reflection of the evolution of thinking process in lexis shows the historical movement from general idea to specialization.

On the basis of historical development of the system of scientific knowledge there distinguished three main periods of evolution of human cognition in anthropolinguistics. They are called pre-scientific period, proto-scientific period and scientific thinking (Grinev-Griniewicz, 2003). The stated chronological terminological layers reveal a range of typical peculiarities. The earliest layer appears on the ground of common words, making polysemy develop. Historical instability of polysemy is explained by different levels of thinking, culture, scientific and machinery development at different stages of mankind evolution. Historical retrospective takes a particular coherent anthropologically based viewpoint to the polysemy. To extract semantic information for the analysis we considered entries in three English dictionaries: Anglo-Saxon Dictionary (ASD), Middle English Dictionary (MED) and Oxford English Dictionary on Historical Principles (OED). Methodology consisted in observation the relations between meanings of polysemous words at different historic periods of language development and the procedure of comparison semantics of one and the same word at different periods.

Anthropolinguistic analysis of polysemous words at separate historical periods followed by aspectual comparing of results reveals dominant tendencies in historical development of interactions between macro-systems. The research of polysemous word as the form of interactions between macro-systems reveals the character of relations in lexical system through different meanings of a word. Historical development of polysemous word may even change the main meaning of a word as in the case with the lexical unit **belly**, the original meaning of which was *a bag, skin-bag, purse, pod, husk* (950). In contemporary English due to the loss of the original meaning **belly** designates *that part of the human body, which lies between the breast and the thighs and contains the bowels; the abdomen* (1340). Having taken the idea of historical character of human cognition and knowledge as methodological base corroborates the hypotheses that historical process of lexis' development follows the ontogenesis scheme.

The word **brow** can exemplify the changes in connections of sign with a variety of objects sharing the shape, function, structure or something else. In the Old English this word had the following meanings: *the fringe of hair along the eye-lid, the eye-lash* (1000) and *the arch of hair over the eye* (1000). These two meanings explicit the initial stage of conceptualization of a fragment of reality. In the Middle English there appeared the meaning *confidence, effrontery* (1642) that shows the development of metonymic associations which were rather common for polysemous words at the historically early stages of language evolution. In due course **brow** became the foundation for developing special lexis, reflecting the formation of proto-scientific thinking. For example, **brow** as *a gallery in a coal-mine running across the face of coal* (1863) is a mining term.

The historical aspect of inner structure of a polysemous word can be analyzed at conceptual level and semantic level as well. The development of semantic categorization registers the evolution of human cognition. Anthropolinguistic research of polysemy shows that the main tendency in knowledge growth is to make the historical impression more precise and detailed.

3.2 Anthropolinguistic Aspect of Metonymy

General features of historic development of English lexis denoting parts of the body show that the character of associative links changes through the stages of evolution of human cognition. Anthropolinguistic approach let us follow the ways of metaphorical and metonymical thinking evolution and hence developing of categorization and conceptualization processes. Diachronic analysis was carried out on the material of the Old English (700–1066), the Middle English (1066–1475), the Early Modern English (1475–1660), the Neoclassical English (1660–1800) and the Late Modern English (1800 – present time). Figure 2 shows the timeline of the stages of the English language.

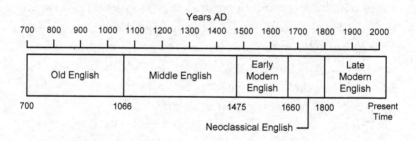

Figure 2. Timeline of the stages of the English language

We shall proceed on the assumption that the issue of re-constructing onomasiological resources over time is possible from the earliest quotations in OED. Still the sources of the English lexis for the analysis are also represented by ASD and MED. The choice of the dictionaries depended on the goal and methods of the investigation.

The use of several reliable dictionaries for the analysis of lexis led to more precise investigation of semantic features of word structure. The semantics of *arm* in the Old English is represented in ASD by the two meanings: *the limb extending from the shoulder to the hand* (950) and *anything projecting from a main body, as an inlet of the sea or ocean* (885). In OED except the above mentioned meanings *arm* is represented by the meaning *might, power, authority* (950). Word is fixed by dictionaries much later than it appears in speech. Thus dictionaries do not give historically correct time of new meaning birth, but let us built word's derivational structure with more precision.

The diachronic analysis shows that in the Old English names of parts of human body had peculiar associations presenting archaic knowledge. In spite of the fact that the semantics of a polysemous word in the Old English is characterized by a vague structure, the historical analysis reveals the features of semantic organisation of the words, denoting parts of the body. For example, *heorte* (heart) – *the hollow muscular or otherwise contractile organ which, by its dilatation and contraction, keeps up the circulation of the blood in the vascular system of an animal* (1000) had the following abstract meanings: *the centre of vital functions: the seat of life; the vital part or principle; hence in some phrases life* (825) *obs.*

or arch.; the seat of courage, hence, courage, spirit (825); *intent, will, purpose, inclination, desire* (825) *obs.* Such meanings are considered to be the result of metonymical associations as they follow the model **part of the body → its manifestation**.

Functional associations with parts of the body gave birth to many syncretic interpretations, connected metonymically. Basic level of cognitive interpretation of reality is named "historic syncretism" (Grinev-Griniewicz, 2003), the term that makes explicit peculiarities of human archaic cognition. Semantic syncretism is defined as non-dismembered unity of different and sometimes even opposite notions. One meaning might combine several abstract notions like the Old English *heorte* (heart) in the meaning *mind in the widest sense including the functions of feelings, volition, and intellect* (825). Semantic structure of the word *heorte* reflects cognitive abilities of a man at that historic time. Word semantics covers wide conceptual space involving different mental and emotional notions that are clearly distinguished in modern dictionaries and cannot be combined in the structure of one word.

The semantics of a polysemous word in the Old English covers a wide field of notions without differentiation of separate ideas. The complexity of a lexical unit may also be the result of unity of adjacent entities like in the case with the word *tunge* (tongue) in the meaning *the faculty of speech; the power of articulation or vocal expression or description; voice; speech; words, language* (890) that is syncretic, since different adjacent notions are revealed in connection with the part of the body. At the same time this meaning is

56

dated earlier than the meaning related to the part of the body – *an organ, possessed by man and by most vertebrates, occupying the floor of the mouth, often protrusible and freely movable* (897).

Human understanding of reality is not chaotic, but based on the knowledge and experience that we have already had. For example, the Old English *hond* (hand) as

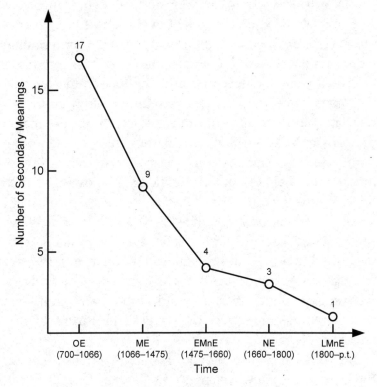

Figure 3. Historical productivity of derivational model
part of the body → its manifestation
(OE – Old English; ME – Middle English; EMnE – Early Modern English;
NE – Neoclassical English; LMnE – Late Modern English)

the terminal part of the arm beyond the wrist, consisting of the palm and five digits (825) motivates the meaning *grasping, possession, keeping, power* (825) that reveals the first functional associations, typical for the initial stage of cognitive evolution. The model **part of the body → its manifestation** is the most representative in the Old English and, definitely, refers to the syncretic metonymic transpositions, since an abstract notion cannot be independent from a concrete one at the earlier stages of evolution of human cognition (Figure 3). Names of parts of the body, representing a prototype category, put anthropolinguistic restrictions to the word semantic development. The foundation for new meanings' appearance is human cognitive activity.

Historical development of semantics within the model **part of the body → its manifestation** leads to the formation of new associations and analogies, caused by the evolution of the field of human knowledge. For example, *limb* develops the meaning *in an isolation or stranded position; at a disadvantage: out on a limb* (1897). New association in the semantics of the word *limb* is caused by the location of the part of the body. In this meaning the notion of periphery as opposed to the centre is associated with *disadvantages*. Semantic derivation fixes the results of human cognition in transferred meanings, creating the basis for further knowledge development.

In the Old English human cognitive activity registers the birth of measure system on the basis of lexis designating parts of the body. At earlier stages of human society development measurement does not have precise character, as measure standards are parts of the body and differ-

58

ent objects. The metonymic model **part of the body** → **measure** defines the concrete and simultaneously diffuse measure system, built on the transition from the name of part of the body to a measure sample. *Fot* (foot) as *the lowest part of the leg beyond the ankle-joint* (745) produces the meaning *a lineal measure originally based on the length of a man's foot (the English foot consists of 12 inches and is 1/3 of a yard)* (1000).

Prototype metonymic model **part of the body** → **measure,** first appeared in the Old English, is getting filled with new units in the Middle English like the unit *schulder* (shoulder) – *each of the two corresponding portions of the human body, including the upper joint of the arm with its integuments and the portion of the trunk between this and the base of the neck* (700) that develops the meaning *to be more, lower by the shoulder* (1300). Alongside with linear measures, dating the Old English period, there appear meanings denoting vertical parameters. In the Morden English such meanings do not designate the measure samples, since they do not denote definite quantitative parameters. However, they are widely used in colloquial speech, reflecting peculiarities of naive picture of the world.

In the Early Modern English there are new units referring to metonymic model **part of the body** → **measure** revealing the experience of the use of weight measures. *Foot* – *the lowest part of the leg beyond the ankle-joint* (745) produces the meaning *a measure in tin-mining* (1602). The definition shows the connection between the measure and the sphere of its application. The use of names of parts of the body for weight measures is due to necessity of creating a unified system of measures. New meanings designating measures in the semantics of the names of parts of the body reveal the historical expansion of human experience in standards of measures.

Names of parts of the body, having features and functions of parts of the body fixed in cognitive experience, expand the English anthroponomical sphere. Actualization of a definite characteristic of a person contributes to formation of a functional layer in the concept PERSON. The metonymic model **part of the body → a human being** is rather scarce in the Old English and is registered by only three units under analysis. For example, *heafod* (head) – *the upper division of the body, joined to the trunk by the neck* (825) motivates anthroponomination *a person to whom others are subordinate; a chief, captain, commander, ruler, leader, principle person* (897).

The diachronic analysis of the metonymic model **part of the body → a human being** registers the development from the general impression of a person to the underlining different aspects in his life. For instance, *lim* (limb) – *a part or member of an animal body distinct from the head or the trunk* (971) motivates the transposition *a social dependent, a liegeman* (1425), denoting social substitution. Later on there appear meanings, which reflect other functions of parts of the body relevant for person like *hand* – *the terminal part of the arm beyond the wrist, consisting of the palm and five digits* (825) in the new transpositions *the person holding the cards* (1589) and *in reference to an artist, musician, writer, actor, as the performer of some work* (1644). The result of motivation combines the idea of *a hand, its functional value* and *a person*.

60

Understanding of oneself through the action is a new stage in the social evolution of a human being. Still the first anthroponomination *a person, individual, agent* (1225) in the semantics of the word *hand* does not detail person's characteristics and gives the most general idea of *functional value of a hand, the act of the action,* while the two mentioned above are connected with the definite situations and skills.

The realisation of a definite functional value leads to the creation of new associations, connected directly with a function of part of the body and to changes within the boundaries of the metonymic model **part of the body → a human being**. For example, *mouth* in the meaning *one who speaks on behalf of another; a spokesman* (1563) forms the base for developing the meanings *a silly person, a dupe* (1680) and *a noisy person* (1700). Historically the ability to speak made a human different from animal world, but then the attention is drawn to estimation aspect of this function. New transferred meanings reveal different associations with the person who speaks much. The appearance of derogatory meanings is connected with a deeper realization of characteristics, which become explicit. Due to the wide spread of drugs and their abuse the word *head* registers the metonymic transposition *a drug-addict* (1911). The meaning is motivated by the realization of influence of drugs on the brain. Thus the well known derivational model undergoes historic modifications, fixing accumulation of adjacent associations.

The greater degree of closeness of elements in the model **part ↔ whole** due to reality allows interpreting it as a specific type of transposition within the frame of derivational metonymic relations, named lexical synecdoche. In this metonymic model there seen a deductive human logic, thanks to which a person is able to extract **part** from **whole**. Because of the human cognitive limits the idea about a referent is not detailed in the Old English that is clear due to semantics of lexis under analysis. At that period the model **part** → **whole** is represented in the semantic structure of one name of parts of the body. *Hela* (heel) – *the projecting hinder part of the foot, below the ankle and behind the hollow of the foot* (850) produces the meaning *applied to the two hind feet, the hoof or the whole foot* (1000). Unproductiveness of the metonymic model **part** ↔ **whole** in the Old English lexis means the lack of the same cognitive category in human cognition. Metonymical expansion of the model **part** ↔ **whole** is the evidence of awareness of hierarchic relations between the elements of reality.

The development of mental category **part** ↔ **whole** is evident in the Middle English, since the productivity of this metonymic model began growing at that period. For example, *bŏdī* (body) – *the main portion of the animal frame, to which the extremities are attached; the trunk* (800) gives birth to the meanings *the belly* (1300), *the waist* (1390) and *the chest* (1400). A number of transferred meanings reveal the understanding of adjacent things and various aspects of this part of the body, its different components. The inductive chain of thoughts explicit in the model **part** → **whole** correlates one part of the body with another bigger in size and including the first one in accordance with the definition. For example, *heorte* (heart) – *the hollow muscular or otherwise contractile organ which, by its dilatation and con-*

traction, keeps up the circulation of the blood in the vascular system of an animal (1000) motivates the meaning *the region of the heart; breast, bosom* (1450).

The development of deductive and inductive principles of thinking and their registration through word semantics reveal the understanding of structure and hierarchy of elements in reality (Figure 4). The appearance of new meanings is possible due to the ongoing process of reality transformation. Inventing new objects and adding them to surroundings people need words to name them. The words

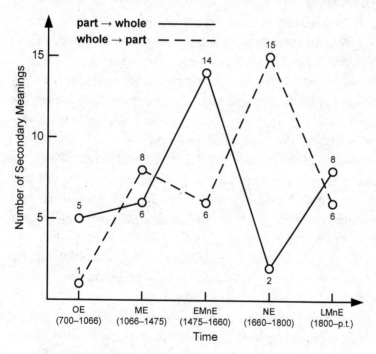

Figure 4. Historical productivity of derivational models
part → whole and **whole → part**

63

that already exist in the language can also suit for presenting new ideas. The derivational metonymic model **whole → part** systematizes new information, using the known conventional structure. So, *side – each of the two grooved faces of a gramophone record* (1936) motivates the meaning *a recording made on the face of a gramophone record, tape recording.*

Since the Middle English period semantics of words under analysis expands due to the use of other metonymic models. Functional value of parts of the body develops thanks to the appearance of new adjacent links according to the model **function → result**. *Eie* (eye) – *with reference to its function: the eye as possessing the power of vision* (1200) forms the base for developing the meaning *opinion or judgment* (1200). *Vision* provides human beings with information about the picture of the world, making the grounds for forming an opinion. The derivational metonymic model **the contained → container** demonstrates the relations between parts of the body and other objects of space. There are different things, which are close to parts of the body in space. *Hele* (heel) – *the projecting hinder part of the foot, below the ankle and behind the hollow of the foot* (850) motivates the meanings *the part of a stocking that covers the heel* (1409) and *the back of a shoe or boot* (1409). Due to this model obvious space adjacent entities of parts of the body are kept in word semantics.

Still there is one more model that also serves for space adjacent relations. It is the model **part of the body → adjacent space**. For example, the word *fot* (foot) – *the lowest part of the leg beyond the ankle-joint* (745) develops the meaning *the end of a bed, a grave towards which the feet are placed* (1300) on the basis of the model **part of the body → adjacent space** and this meaning is still relevant in the language. Metonymic transposition in the words referring to parts of the body may correlate not only with the definite entity from surroundings, but also with the space around a person in general. A vivid example can be the word *nose* that has the meaning *closeness or proximity to a person or thing* (1526). In this case the closeness to the person is not denoted by the objects, which can vary, but by one of the parts of his body.

Being carnivorous people use parts of animals' body as food and it has also been revealed in the semantics of lexical units designating parts of the body since the Middle English period. So, the model **part of the body → food** is observed in *tongue* (tongue) – *an organ, possessed by man and by most vertebrates, occupying the floor of the mouth, often protrusible and freely movable* (897) which produces the meaning *the tongue of an animal as an article of food* (1420). Many other words motivate transferred secondary meanings using this model later.

In the Late Modern English there appeared a new metonymic model **function → object**. This can be traced in the semantics of the word *ear* – *the sense of hearing, auditory perception* (825) → *a citizen's-band radio, its antenna or the vehicle carrying* (1976). The word semantics fixes the link between the *auditory perception* and a definite sound resource. As a result of semantic evolution of words denoting parts of the body not only onomasiological aspect of the word develops, but semasiological one as well.

The analysis shows that metonymic categories are different. Basic metonymic categories like **part ↔ whole** stay actual in any historic period of language evolution. For example, in the Early Modern English there appear a number of meanings denoting *the amount of people* and the basis for this kind of transition is still the metonymic model **part → whole**. The process of this model development results in the meanings with a conjunctive unity of ideas about *part of the body, its function* and *an amount of people*. For example, **head** gets the meaning *a body of people gathered; a force raised, esp. in insurrection* (1588).

The development of existing lexical items involves both extension and obsolescence. Obsolescence, in its turn, leads to reorganization of the word structure. So, **heart** has lost the meaning *intent, will, purpose, inclination, desire* (825) *obs.* that is explained by the loss of associations between these notions and the part of the body. The process of obsolescence of some of the word's meanings gets a new explanation. It is caused by better understanding of the surroundings. We may say that the obsolescence promotes updating of word semantics. At the same time some of the obsolete meanings may be still used in phraseological units as *by heart* is motivated by the meaning *memory* (950), which is not fixed in modern dictionaries any more. The development of human cognition presented in the language is a historically long period. Knowledge evolution can lead to the substitution of one semantic fragment with another, while some archaic associations can still remain in the language as transformed ones.

Historical retrospective of the words denoting parts of

the body reveals that in the Old English period there were only three more metonymic models except **part ↔ whole: part of the body → its manifestation, part of the body → measure, part of the body → a human being**. In the Middle English period there appear new metonymic models such as **container → the contained, function → result** and **part of the body → food, part of the body → adjacent space** registered in dictionaries. And then only one more metonymic model **function → object** appears in the Late Modern English.

On the other hand, historical retrospective analysis reveals a gradually descending scale of diachronic productivity of metonymic models in comparison with metaphoric models. Hence the obvious prevalence of metonymic associations in semantics of words denoting parts of the body in the Old English is then changed by metaphorization in the Late Modern English.

3.3 Anthropolinguistic Aspect of Metaphor

Anthropolinguistic view on the words designating parts of the body reveals main tendencies of the development of metaphorical thinking as an essential part of human cognition. Metaphor is able to make different associative grounds of a polysemous word explicit. The transferred meaning created on the base of a word denoting a part of the body can then develop new associations and hence motivate the representation of new notions in word structure. Modification of semantics in definite meanings is possible due to redistribution and new combinations of the already known semantic material.

Metaphorical changes were not typical in the Old English and that is why, they were very numerous at that period and reflected the most vivid characteristics of parts of human body. For example, *muþ* (mouth) – *the exterior opening or orifice of the mouth considered as part of the face* (900) gives birth to the meaning *opening, orifice of things* (1000). The symbol of metaphor in this case is the idea of *opening*. Visual properties of parts of human body define the basic stage in semantic metaphorization.

Metaphorical model **part of the body → part of a natural object** marks not the case of anthropocentrism at the early stage of language development, but defines a human being as a part of nature. Metaphorical transitions of that period had their specific features. Thus metaphorical model **part of a natural object → part of the body** is characteristic for the Old English only and is not registered by any other historical periods. *Nosu* (nose) – *a ness, a piece of land projecting into water* (VII–VIII centuries) motivated the meaning *that part (usually more or less prominent) of the head or face in humans and animals which lies above the mouth and contains the nostrils* (897). Regarding himself as a fragment of the world and the absence of opposition between a human being and nature can be stated as "historic syncretism". This is also observed in the word *earm* (arm) with the meanings *a narrow portion or part of the sea projecting from the main body* (885) and *the upper limb of the human body, from the shoulder to the hand* (950). The metaphorical basis revealed in a word structure reflects the limit of possibilities of human cognition at a definite historic period. In semantics of polysemous lexical units of that time the part of metaphorically transferred meanings forms only half of metonymically motivated meanings.

In the Middle English metaphorical shift of the meaning is caused by more precise understanding of visual peculiarities of the body. As a result new transposition does not leave the sphere of parts of the body, but reveals some conventional characteristics of parts of the body. As an example, **bak** (back) – *the convex surface of the body of man and vertebrate animals which is adjacent to the spinal axis, and opposite to the belly and the front or face* (885) gives birth to the meaning *the outer side of the hand or finger, opposite to the palm* (1300). *The location* of part of the body is one of the first metaphorical grounds for the meaning shift. The analogy within the same field of knowledge can be seen as the starting point in the mastery of cognitive mechanisms.

The metaphorical model **part of the body** → **part of a natural object** reveals new interpretation of relations between a human being and nature. The dynamics of mastery of metaphorical potential of a word reveals further development of visual thinking. *Earm* (arm) – *the upper limb of the human body, from the shoulder to the hand* (950) forms the basis for the meaning *one of the limbs of a river, a nerve, or the like* (1330). Anthropolinguistic development of the metaphor symbol in transferred meanings of the word *arm* registers schematization and working out the visual image of the referent in detail in the Middle English. The transferred meaning shows that the word semantics fixes *the location* of *arms* at the both sides of the body for the first time.

Language metaphorization of facts of reality is not always characterized by the prevalence of *visual* and *spatial* analogy. At the same time it is clear that visual perception forms the basis for further transferences and creating new associations. Polymorphic structure of metaphor symbol does not do without explication of visual peculiarities of parts of the body. Functional characteristic of part of the body becomes one of the components of the complex association. So, the complex of the three components (visual analogy, spatial characteristic, function similarity) is revealed in a number of units in the Middle English like *foot* in the meaning *the leg of a bench, chair, table* (1387) produced on the base of the meaning *the entire leg.*

Since the Middle English in some metaphorical transitions *functional* analogy has been realized alone. For instance, **muþ** (mouth) – *the exterior opening or orifice of the mouth considered as part of the face* (900) motivates the meaning *a strait leading to a sea; the entrance to a harbour* (1325). The transferred meaning does not reveal any *visual* analogy, but being *the entrance* means understanding of the way *the mouth* is used. Immanent evolution of idea requires the modification of the mechanism of information collection. Functional value of part of the body is fixed in word semantics as a relevant component in the familiarization of a fragment of reality.

Word semantics shows the ongoing process of reality articulation and changes in the original interpretation of reality. On the basis of historic meanings there is specialization observed in the narrowing of semantics in transferred meanings and the registration of new metaphorical grounds, manifesting realization of other characteristics of parts of the body. A human being is becoming more interested in details, which were not essential for him earlier and, consequently, were not explicit in the lexical system of the language. Cognitive evolution of mankind determines the expansion of semantic links providing the evolution of polysemy.

New components in word semantics make explicit gradual changes in basic ideas like in the case with *eye – the organ of sight in man and vertebrate animals* (700), which produces the meaning *an orifice or perforation, as the eye of a needle, the hole in a millstone, a hole in cheese* (1225) in the Middle English. This shift happened thanks to the association with *the round shape of the eye*. The meaning *slight shade, tinge* (1610) observed in the Early Modern English reveals a new associative ground. Semantics of the transferred meaning registers the association with *colour* characteristic of *the organ of sight*. The denoted characteristic becomes abstract from the definite bearer and can be applied to any object of reality.

In the Neoclassical English the evolution of polysemy of units denoting parts of the body is determined by the change of correlation of the shares between metaphorically motivated meanings and metonymic derivatives in the structure of polysemous words. The quantitative reduction of metonymic transpositions in comparison with earlier historic periods is determined by the limited number of adjacent associations, built on the analogy by word semantics. Later on semantic modifications are connected not so much with the registration of adjacent relations, but rather with the metaphorical associations' development.

Conceptual transpositions, traditionally motivated by metonymic models, are then added by metaphorical shifts. Thus measure system on the basis of words denoting parts of the body, represented earlier by the models **part of the body → measure** and **part → whole**, develops new metaphorical models. For example, *head – as a unit in numbering cattle, game* (1513) and *a person in enumeration* (1535) produces the meaning *a bundle of flax or silk* (1704). The new meaning reveals rather functional association than visual analogy with the part of the body. Original use of the word *head* for the counting of animals and people let realise the same model of derivation with other objects of reality which require counting.

The development of metaphorical thinking makes the ground for creating functional associations on the base of visual images. *Arm – one of the branches into which a main trunk divides. esp. of a vine* (1398) motivates the meaning *an administrative branch; a division of a company or organization*. The original visual perception in the historical meaning gives birth to logical statements, connected with deduction. Judicial dependence of *administrative branches* and their hierarchical organization are equalled to *visual* characteristics of branches in a tree structure.

Alongside with the developing of functional association anthropolinguistic approach reveals further splitting of semantics of metaphor grounds in the Modern English language. For example, the unity of *shape* and *location* characteristics in the symbol of metaphor typical for metaphorical transitions at earlier historical stages is not registered in the language as well as other metaphors with a number of characteristics in its symbol. The greatest number of components in metaphor symbol for the words under analysis is three and it is found in the Middle English and no more later.

The only one polysemous symbol of metaphor in the Modern English language is the unity of *shape* and *function* characteristics. For example, the polysemous word **tongue** realises the meaning *a narrow and deep part of the current of a river, running smoothly and rapidly between rocks* (1891). The analogy of *the shape* and *the movement of the tongue in the mouth* are used by conscious for language representation of nature entity. Most of the meanings are motivated by only one characteristic like in the word **foot** – *the lowest part of the leg beyond the ankle-joint* (745), which motivates the meaning *lower edge of a sail* (1697) due to the peculiarities of *location* that is traced through the words *lowest* and *lower*.

Cognitive nature of metaphorical processes determines further semantic reorganization of polysemous words under analysis. Multiple applications to the part of the body give birth to further modifications in the system of notions. Seeing one object through many others reveals the development of semantic components in word semantics. For example, **shank** develops the meaning *a short rope or chain* (1706), which is motivated by the analogy of the *size of part of the body*. The perception of **shank** – *that part of the leg which extends from the knee to the ankle* through *the size* is a new aspect of categorization, not registered by word semantics earlier.

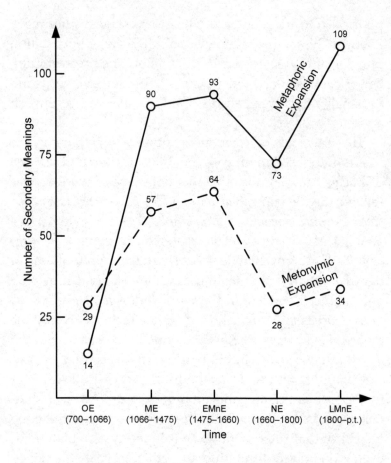

Figure 5. Semantic evolution of the words denoting parts of the body

The development of scientific knowledge, being more advanced level of evolution of human cognition, is also revealed in the semantics of polysemous words. New meanings of specialized character still trace the links with common knowledge. For example, physical characteristics of part of the body can be used as the basis for presenting scientific notions in the language. Hence *body* produces the meaning *any kind of substance, simple or compound, solid or liquid or gaseous* (1594), which is used in chemistry. Then, in due course of time, there appeared a more specialized meaning *that which has sensible qualities or as perceptible by the senses; matter; substance* (1668). The second meaning applies not to the kind of substance, but rather to the way it is seen by a human and in this case it contributes to the idea of detailed presentation of the surroundings. Both meanings denote the same referent, but they are different in the way they present it in the language.

The analysis shows that some of the metaphorical meanings became obsolete due to the changes in the conceptual information as the word basis. Thus *nose* is not used in the meaning *an elephant's trunk obs.* (1601) that is explained by realization of the difference between this part of the face in human and in animal. Historically these notions were united in the semantics of one word, but later the visual peculiarities of *an elephant's trunk* encouraged the semantic transmission from one phonetic form to another with the more suitable associations. The extracted obsolete meanings of the names of the parts of the body (Appendix) make explicit lost associations.

On the whole, the metaphoric expansion of semantics of words denoting parts of the body reveals a higher growth rate through history in contrast to the metonymic evolution (Figure 5). It is more typical for the Present Day English to use metaphor associations to create a new meaning on the base of the words denoting parts of the body.

3.4 Terms

Terms are different from words as they are used in special subject domains. Terms belong to language for specific purposes (LSP) while words are used in language for general purposes (LGP), also called sublanguage. With the development of specialized fields of knowledge polysemous word demonstrates the operability to include terminological meanings (terms) in its semantics. Due to the interests of lexicographers and translators the semantic information of a word occurs split in common and special dictionaries. Thus to observe the semantics of a polysemous word today you need to extract the information from several lexicographic resources. Terminological meanings reveal the same associations as common ones. For example, *neck – the back part of that portion of the body lying between the head and shoulders* (897) produces the term *the columns of cooled lava which fill up an old volcanic chimneys* (1876) that is used in volcanology and geology. The terminological meaning shows the analogy of *shape* and *location* between **neck** as part of the body and a new special referent.

Neological processes or terminologization in polysemy activates semantic elements that have been already shared by earlier meanings of the word or, and this is the most essential moment, new semantic elements that actually define anthropological tendency. So the word **heart** develops the meaning that refers to mechanics *a heart-shaped wheel or cam used for converting a rotary into a reciprocating motion* (1875) that is motivated not only by the *shape* of the referent, but also the idea of the work of a heart as *the organ* *that keeps up blood circulation.* Thus the associations are becoming more precise, definite and deep throughout the evolution of the mankind.

Cognitive transformation of information modifies the existent semantics of a polysemantic word, creating new analogies, which account for associative character of scientific thinking. Thus **body** in the mathematical meaning *a figure of three dimensions; a solid regular body: one of the five Regular Solids* (1570) makes the semantic information of the word more detailed due to the evolution of scientific knowledge of the world. The definition shows some definite characteristics like *three dimensions, solid* which are of particular interest for mathematics.

Specialized meanings appeared on the basis of semantics of the names of parts of the body manifest *visual* and *logical* associations as well. Specifity of word's semantics in the definite field of knowledge accounts for a special field of its usage. For example, the word **arm** developed the specialized meaning in machinery: *of a balance of machines, in a lever: the part or length from the fulcrum to the point of application of the power or weight respectively* (1659) that is associated with the *function* of this part of the body. The same word in the meaning *the parts of the yard extending on either side of the mast; Yard-Arm* (1665) used in a different sphere of knowledge reveals the *visual* analogy between the original meaning and a specialized one.

With the development of medicine people find out new parts in human body and use the words, which have already had the reference to the parts of the body. These new meanings are known for only specialists while ordinary people do not have an idea about them. Here is a good example with the word *knee* – *the part of the limb; the joint, or region about the joint between the thigh and the lower leg* (825) that now has the meaning *in the brain the part of the corpus callosum that bends* (1840), where we can observe *visual* analogy. These new parts in a human body are small in size and require advanced knowledge to be found.

Gradual differentiation of special knowledge is seen in the historical increase of number of special fields of knowledge presented in the semantic structure of the polysemous words under analysis. First special marks, limiting the sphere of meaning use, date back to the Middle English. Special fields of knowledge of that period were predominantly connected with different kinds of manufacture and first sciences. For example, the word *back* in the meaning *the thickest and best-tanned hides* (1535) refers to leather manufacture. Also typical for that period were meanings concerning medicine like the word *mouth* in the meaning *the external opening of a sore, wound, ulcer, hemorrhoid* (1398). A human being was gradually learning more and more about himself and his body and also about surroundings. So the word *heel* produces the meaning *the hinder toe or hallux in birds, the spur* (1611) which is motivated by a complex of analogies of *location* and *shape*.

Development of scientific knowledge is traced through the appearance of new meanings belonging to scientific fields of knowledge. For example, the word *head* develops the meaning *the commencement of a zodiacal sign, the point where the sun enters it* (1200) that refers to the astrology. The word *nose* produced the term *the beak or rostrum of an alem-*

bic, retort or still (1651) that is used in chemistry. The word *foot* enters the sphere of geometry in the terminological meaning *foot of the perpendicular* (1840). The lexical unit *limb* develops the terminological meaning *a member or a clause of a sentence (1863)* used in linguistics.

There are plenty of secondary meanings of the words under analysis in the sphere of ship building like *shank* in the meaning *the shaft or stem of an anchor, connecting the arms and the stalk* (1549). Possessing different characteristics part of the body can be referred to for several times to represent special knowledge in one and the same sphere. For example, *heart* in the transferred meaning *a triangular wooden block pierced with one large hole through which a lanyard is reeved, used for extending the stays; a kind of dead-eye* (1769) is based on the *shape* of the part of the body. *Heart* in the terminological meaning *the central strand of a hawser-laid rope, round which the other strands are twisted* (1841) appeals to the meaning *the centre of vital functions* (825) and hence reflects the relevance of *location*.

Through the secondary meanings one can observe the history of some particular sphere of life. The meanings referred to the sphere of building and architecture reveal the peculiarities of buildings like the word *neck* in the meaning *the narrow part of a bastion or embrasure* (1668) that demonstrates the military character of the nomination. The lexical unit *shoulder* also presents a part of fortification in the meaning *epauler, the place of a bastion where the face and flank meet* (1702). Then *shank* in the meaning *pl. the plane spaces between the grooves of the Doric triglyph* (1823) correlates with the notion of the definite architectural order.

The diachronic analysis on the basis of lexicographic resources demonstrates that polysemous words denoting parts of the body, nineteen in number, enter more than sixty special fields of knowledge. Specialization is gradually becoming the main way of polysemy development in words under analysis. The studied polysemous words reveal the prevalence of metaphor associations in terminological meanings. Semantic modifications that register special knowledge in structure of the polysemous words are determined by both *visual* and *rational* characteristics of parts of the body. Metonymic transference is typical for medical and sports terminological meanings only like the word *side* in the metonymic meaning *in billiards direction given to a ball by striking it at a point not directly in the middle* (1873).

Conclusion

We would like to note that the observations undertaken demonstrate that polysemy can be studied from the perspective of mankind evolution that is still going on regarding not morphological features of a human being this time, but his mental abilities, way of thinking, and advanced level of knowledge. The research touches the study of national cognitive peculiarities, and we can compare the language picture of the world at different historic periods. The studied historical differences and the similarities of word semantics allow us to state the two main tendencies in its development:

a) semantic extension clarifies the developing ability of a human being to realize new facts and aspects of a well known referent;
b) obsolescence accounts for the changes in associations that leads to better understanding of reality.

Appendix

The List of the Obsolete Meanings, Extracted from the Dictionaries Compared

Arm:

1) One of the branches into which a main trunk divides esp. of a vine obs. (1398);
2) Anat. the Fallopian tube (1425);
3) Land, mountain resembling arm obs. (1538).

Back:

1) A garment which covers the back; a cloak, pl. clothes obs. (1250);
2) A person's back as covered by clothing or armour (1300);
3) The waist (1390);
4) Limb, organ, tissue (1398);
5) The chest (1400);
6) Armour protecting the back; a back-plate obs. (1648);
7) Of time: the other side of, the time after obs. (1673);
8) A following; a body of followers or supporters; support, backing obs. (1566).

Body:

1) The seven ancient metals answering to the seven "heavenly bodies" obs. (1386);
2) Substance as opposed to representation, shadow; reality obs. (1382);
3) The vessel in which a substance to be distilled is placed; a retort obs. (1559);
4) Geom. a figure of three dimensions obs. (1570);
5) An entity, a thing which has real existence; an agent or cause of phenomena obs. (1587);
6) The wood under the bark obs. (1603).

Ear:

1) With adj. or noun modifiers describing the receptiveness or disposition of the person listening (1225);
2) One of the auricles of the heart obs. (1398);
3) *Sleep on the right ear*: to sleep lying on one side obs. (1663);
4) Used in the description of a Roman plough obs. (1697).

Eye:

1) *In (the) eye*: in appearance obs. (1394);
2) The knee-cap (1398);
3) Range of vision, view, sight obs. (1599);
4) A fountain or spring obs. (1609);
5) Slight shade, tinge obs. (1610);
6) Hydrophane. The eye of the world obs. (1672).

Foot:

1) Viewed with regard to its function, as the organ of locomotion denotes the kind of movement (1000);
2) A person as walking obs. (1200);
3) Used to express the least distance or space obs. (1290);
4) That one of the parts of a tripartite indenture recording the particulars of a fine which remained with the court, the other two being retained by the parties (1293);
5) Power of walking or running obs. (1300);
6) A part of a plough, a device attached to the beam of a plough to regulate the depth of the ploughing (1325);
7) The sum of total (of an account) obs. (1433);
8) The whole limb from the hip-joint to the toes obs. (1541);
9) The refrain or "chorus" of a song obs. (1552);
10) The footing, basis, understanding totality of conditions or arrangements on which a matter is established or status which a person or thing occupies in relation to another (1559);
11) Foothold, standing-ground obs. (1579);
12) Standard rate of calculation or valuation obs. (1588).

Hand:

1) Used in various ways in making an oath or asservation obs. (1300);
2) A fight, battle, assault, attack (1382);
3) Strength, valour, fighting ability, fighting spirit (1385);
4) An armed band (1460);
5) Position, case obs. (1489);

6) A handle obs. (1523);
7) The name of a person written with his own hand as an attestation of a document obs. (1534);
8) A person as supplier of goods obs. (1552);
9) The trunk of an elephant obs. (1607);
10) A person as a source of information obs. (1614);
11) The whole arm obs. (1615).

Head:

1) The beginning of a word or writing obs. (1200);
2) The commencement of a zodiacal sign obs. (1200);
3) An end, extremity of a stone, brick obs. (1400);
4) The hair as dressed in some particular manner obs. (1494);
5) The capital of a column obs. (1552);
6) A body of people gathered; a force raised esp. in insurrection obs. (1588);
7) Turning of the head, backward change of the course obs. (1607).

Heart:

1) Considered as the centre of vital functions: the seat of life; the vital part or principle; hence in some phrases = life obs. or arch. (825);
2) Intent, will, purpose, inclination, desire obs. (825);
3) Disposition, temperament, character obs. (1225);
4) The sole of a horse's foot obs. (1523);

5) The vital, essential, or efficacious part: essence (often combined with other notions) obs. (1533);
6) The stomach obs. or dial. Chiefly in phrases next the heart: on an empty stomach, fasting (1542);
7) The feeling or sentiment which one has in regard to a thing obs. (1596);
8) As a term of compassion: poor heart obs. (1599);
9) Dear heart: a boon companion. obs. (1663).

Heel:

1) Put for the foot as a whole (1225).

Knee:

1) A degree of descent in a genealogy obs. (1000);
2) The kneecap, patella (1400);
3) An articulation or joint; esp. a bent joint in some grasses obs. (1597).

Limb:

1) An agent or scion of the evil one; an imp of Satan (971);
2) Any organ or part of the body obs. (1000);
3) In uses originally fig. A member (e.g. of the church as the body of Christ, of Christ, of Antichrist); a branch or section; an element or component part obs. (1000);
4) Refer inclusively to all the bodily faculties: *life and limb, limb and land* (1205);
5) An estate, etc. dependent on another obs. (1442);

6) Applied to things obs. (1593);
7) The pieces of a suit of armour obs. (1651).

Mouth:

1) By mouth: by spoken words, orally, often opposed to "by writing" (1330);
2) A person's utterance obs. (1400);
3) What pertains to the providing and preparing of food for the king: *the king's mouth* obs. (1433);
4) One who speaks on behalf of another; a spokesman obs. (1563);
5) *To draw one's mouth*: to extract a tooth obs. (1669).

Neck:

1) The setting on of an assailant, the imposition of some burden, or the laying of a charge upon a person obs. (1536);
2) Inexactly used for head obs. (1560);
3) *To break the neck of*: to destroy, finish, bring to an end obs. (1576).

Nose:

1) A socket on a candlestick, into which the lower end of the candle is inserted, a projecting doorway obs. (1400);
2) Applied to an elephant's trunk obs. (1601);
3) In gluing up a volume, if the workman has not been careful to make all the sheets occupy a right line at the head, it will present a point called a nose (1865).

Shank:

1) Pl. a kind of fur obtained from the legs of animals, esp. kids, goats or sheep, used for trimming outer garments obs. (1400);
2) The tunnel of a chimney obs. (1525);
3) The stem of a candlestick obs. (1577);
4) Each of the "legs" of a pair of compasses. Also each of the "legs" of a triangle obs. (1587);
5) The neck of a still or alembic obs. (1600);
6) The upper part of the leg (Old English).

Side:

1) Used with reference to generation or birth obs. (900);
2) The outskirts of a wood, town, etc. obs. (1300);
3) In other sides obs. (1340);
4) On side obs. (1375);
5) One of the two divisions of a choir obs. (1519);
6) A page of a book or writing obs. (1530);
7) Math. Root (1660).

Tongue:

1) In a biblical use: a people or nation having a language of their own. Usually in pl. (1382);
2) The pole of a wagon or other vehicle; the head of a plough obs. (1591);
3) A voice, vote, suffrage obs. rare (1607);
4) Eulogy, fame obs. rare (1616);

5) In fortification, a pointed horn-work obs. (1688);
6) A wedge, an ingot of gold or silver obs. (1535).

References

ALLWOOD, J. (2003). Meaning potentials and context: Some consequences for the analysis of variation in meaning. In: Cuyckens, H., Dirven, R., & Taylor, J. R. (Eds). *Cognitive Approaches to Lexical Semantics*. Berlin, New York: Mouton de Gruyter, pp. 29-67.

APRESJAN, J. D. (1974). Regular polysemy. *Linguistics*, 142, pp. 5-32.

BACHERLARD, G. (1978). *Die Bildung des wissenschaftlichen Geistes - Beitrag zu einer Psychoanalyse der objektiven Erkenntnis*. Frankfurt: Suhrkamp.

BECH, G. (1951). Grundzüge der semantischen Entwicklungsgeschiche der hochdeutschen Modalverba. In: *Historisk-filologiske Meddelelser*. Det Kongelige Danske Videnskabernes Selskab, 32(6), pp. 1-28.

BICKERTON, D. (1969). Prolegomena to a linguistic theory of metaphor. *Foundations of Language*, 5, pp. 34-52.

BLACK, M. (1962). *Models and Metaphor. Studies in Language and Philosophy.* Ithaca: Cornell University Press.

BLOOMFIELD, L. (1933). *Language.* New York: Allen & Unwin.

BOSWORTH, J. (1973). *Anglo-Saxon Dictionary.* Oxford: Oxford University Press.

BREAL, M. (1924). *Essai de sémantique (Science des significations).* Reprint of the 4th ed. Paris: Gerard Monfort.

CASSIRER, E. (1977). *Philosophie der symbolischen Formen.* Darmstadt: Wissenschaft Buchgesellschaft

CORSON, D. (1995). *Using English Words.* Dordrecht, Boston: Kluwer Academics Publishers.

COSERIU, E. (1974). *Synchronie, Diachronie und Geschichte: Das Problem des Sprachwandels.* Internationale Bibliothek für allgemeine Linguistik. München: Fink.

CRUSE, D. A. (1993). Between polysemy and monosemy: Senses, facets and qualia roles. In: *Proceedings of the International Conference on New Trends in Semantics and Lexicography.* Kazimierz, Poland, December 13-15, 1993. Umea: Swedish Science Press, pp. 25-35.

FOLEY, W. (1997). *Anthropological Linguistics: An Introduction.* Oxford: Blackwell.

GEERAERTS, D. (1997). *Diachronic Prototype Semantics: A Contribution to Historical Lexicology.* Oxford: Clarendon Press.

GOODMAN, N. (1981). Metaphor as moonlighting. In: Johnson, M. (Ed). *Philosophical Perspectives on Metaphor*. Minneapolis: Minnesota University Press, pp. 221-227.

GRINEV-GRINIEWICZ, S. (2003). Terminological foundations of reasoning: Towards the general theory of evolution of human knowledge. *Terminology Science & Research*, 14, pp. 41-51.

HORNBY, A. S. (2007). *Oxford Advanced Leaner's Dictionary of Current English*. Oxford, New York: Oxford University Press.

JACKSON, H. & AMVELA, E. Z. (2000). *Words, Meaning and Vocabulary: An Introduction to Modern English Lexicology*. Open Linguistics Series. London, New York: Cassell.

JANSSEN, T. (2003). Monosemy versus polysemy. In: Cuyckens, H., Dirven, R., Taylor J. R. & Langacker, R. W. (Eds). *Cognitive Approaches to Lexical Semantics*. Cognitive Linguistics Research, 23. Berlin: Walter de Gruyter, pp. 93-122.

KILGARRIFF, A. & GAZDAR, G. (1995). Polysemous relations. In: Palmer, F. (Ed). *Grammar and Meaning: Essays in Honour of Sir John Layons*. Cambridge: Cambridge University Press, pp. 1-25.

KURATH, H. (Ed). (1954). *Middle English Dictionary*. Ann Arbor: University of Michigan.

LAKOFF, G. (1987). *Women, Fire and Other Dangerous Things: What Categories Reveal About the Mind*. Chicago: University of Chicago Press.

LANGAKER, R. W. (1968). *Language and its Structure: Some Fundamental Linguistic Concepts*. New York: Harcourt, Brace & World.

LEHRER, A. & LEHRER, K. (1995). Fields, networks and vectors. In: Palmer, F. (Ed*). Grammar and Meaning: Essays in Honour of Sir John Layons*. Cambridge: Cambridge University Press, pp. 26-47.

LLOYD, S. M. (Ed). (1982). *Roget's Thesaurus of English Words and Phrases*. Harlow: Longman House.

LYONS, J. (1995). *Language and Linguistics: An Introduction*. Cambridge, New York: Cambridge University Press.

MCELHINNY, B., HOLS, M., HOLTZKENER, J., UNGER, S. & HICKS, C. (2003). Gender, publication and citation in sociolinguistics and linguistic anthropology: The construction of a scholarly canon. *Language in Society*, 32(3), pp. 299-328.

MCKNIGHT, G. H. (1923). *English Words and their Background*. New York, London: D. Appleton and Co.

MEDNIKOVA, E. M. & APRESIAN, Y. D. (1993). *New English-Russian Dictionary*. Moscow: Russkiy Yazik.

MILLER, G. A. (1993). Images and models, similes and metaphors. In: Ortony, A. (Ed). *Metaphor and Thought*. 2nd Ed. Cambridge: Cambridge University Press, pp. 357-400.

OGATA, H. A. (1942). *Dictionary of English Homonyms, Pronouncing and Explanatory*. Tokyo: Maruzen Company.

OGDEN, C. K. & RICHARDS, I. A. (1946). *The Meaning of Meaning: A Study of the Influence of Language upon Thought and of the Science of Symbolism.* 8th Ed. New York: Harcourt, Brace & World.

PIAGET, J. (1926). *The Language and Thought of the Child.* New York: Harcourt, Brace & Company, Inc.

PIERCE, C. S. (1958). *Collected Papers of Charles Sanders Peirce, Volumes VII and VIII, Science and Philosophy and Reviews, Correspondence and Bibliography.* Cambridge: Harvard University Press.

RICHARDS, L. A. (1936). *The Philosophy of Rhetoric.* New York: Oxford University Press.

ROSCH, E. (1977). Human categorization. In: Warren, N. (Ed). *Advances in Cross-Cultural Psychology,* 1. London: Academic Press, 1-72.

RYLE, G. (1949). *The Concept of Mind.* New York: Barnes & Noble.

SHORE, B. (1990). Twice-born, one conceived: meaning-construction and cultural cognition. *American Anthropologist,* 93(1), pp 9-27.

SIMPSON, J. A. & WEINER, E. S. C. (Eds). (1989). *Oxford English Dictionary.* 2nd Ed. Oxford: Clarendon Press.

SKEAT, W. (1909). *An Etymological Dictionary of the English Language.* Oxford: Clarendon Press.

STERN, G. (1964). *Meaning and Change of Meaning, with Special Reference to the English Language*. Bloomington: Indiana University Press.

STEVICK, R. D. (1968). *English and its History: The Evolution of a Language*. Boston: Allyn and Bacon.

TRIER, J. (1931). *Der deutsche Wortschatz im Sinnbezirk des Verstandes: Von den Anfangen bis zum Beginn des 13 Jahrhunderts*. Heidelberg: C. Winter.

TURNER, M. & FAUCONNIER, G. (2000). Metaphor, metonymy and binding. In: Barcelona, A. (Ed). *Metaphor and Metonymy at the Crossroads: A Cognitive Perspective*. Topics in English Linguistics, 30. The Hague: Mouton de Gruyter, pp. 133-145.

ULLMANN, S. (1957). *The Principles of Semantics*. Glasgow University Publications, 84. Glasgow: Jackson, Son & Co.

ULLMANN, S. (1962). *Semantics: An Introduction to the Science of Meaning*. Oxford: Blackwell.

Notes

Notes